Introduction

In the intricate world of dental clinic management, one fundamental truth stands above all: **cash flow is king.** It is the lifeblood that sustains your clinic's operations, allowing you to provide the highest quality dental care, support your dedicated staff, and keep the lights on. However, mastering the ebb and flow of financial resources within a dental practice is no simple feat.

In this book, we delve into the heart of the matter, exploring the art and science of managing cash flow in a dental clinic. Whether you're an experienced Dental Finance Manager or a newcomer to the field, the principles and strategies shared here will equip you with the knowledge and tools needed to navigate this critical aspect of your role.

We will begin by dissecting the essence of cash flow management, understanding why it is paramount, and exploring the implications of suboptimal financial stewardship. Then, we'll journey through a maze of strategies designed to ensure a consistent flow of funds into your clinic, even when faced with the most challenging circumstances.

The financial health of your dental clinic is not just a matter of number crunching; it's about ensuring the well-being of your patients, the stability of your staff, and the enduring success of your practice. So, let's embark on this essential financial odyssey and learn to master dental clinic cash flow.

Written By **Dr. P. Mohan Raju**

Chapter 1 - Understand the Importance of Cash Flow

Cash flow is the lifeblood of any business, and a dental clinic is no exception. Understanding the importance of cash flow is the first step towards mastering it. Cash flow refers to the movement of money into and out of your dental clinic, and it is crucial for several reasons:

1. Operational Sustainability: Cash flow is what keeps your dental clinic operational. It allows you to pay for essential day-to-day expenses, such as staff salaries, rent, utilities, and supplies. Without a healthy cash flow, you risk not being able to meet these obligations, which can disrupt your clinic's operations.

2. Investment and Growth: Cash flow is the source of funds for investments and expansions. It enables you to purchase new equipment, renovate your clinic, or hire additional staff. Without a stable cash flow, your ability to invest in your clinic's growth is severely limited.

Here is an example to make it more clear for you

Meet Dr. A and Dr. B, both experienced dentists with their own dental clinics in the same town.

Dr. A's clinic, "Smile Bright Dental," has a steady stream of patients, and he's known for his excellent patient care. However, his cash flow management has been somewhat lax. He hasn't allocated funds for emergencies or planned for clinic expansion. One day, an opportunity arises to purchase the latest digital imaging equipment that could greatly enhance diagnostic capabilities and improve patient experiences. Dr. A is interested, but his limited cash flow makes it difficult to invest in the new equipment without compromising his clinic's daily operations.

Dr. B, on the other hand, runs the "Healthy Smiles Dental Clinic." He has been diligent in managing his clinic's cash flow. He maintains a financial buffer for unforeseen expenses and has developed a robust budget that factors in investments and growth opportunities. When he hears about the opportunity to invest in the latest dental technology, Dr. B is well-prepared. His stable cash flow allows him to confidently make the purchase, knowing that it won't disrupt his clinic's operations. The new equipment quickly sets his clinic apart, attracting more patients and enhancing the quality of care he provides.

In this scenario, Dr. B's proactive cash flow management has given him the financial flexibility to seize growth opportunities and invest in his clinic's advancement. Dr. A, while an excellent dentist, faces limitations in his ability to invest and expand due to his less stable cash flow. The story underscores the importance of cash flow as the lifeblood of a dental clinic's potential for investment and growth.

3.Risk Mitigation: A strong cash flow acts as a financial safety net. It helps your clinic weather unexpected financial challenges or emergencies, such as equipment breakdowns or unforeseen economic downturns. Having a financial buffer in the form of cash reserves can prevent your clinic from facing financial crises.

4. Credibility: Consistent cash flow demonstrates your clinic's financial stability to creditors, suppliers, and potential investors. It enhances your clinic's credibility and makes it easier to secure financing or negotiate favourable terms with vendors.

5. Flexibility and Decision-Making: A steady cash flow provides you with the flexibility to make strategic decisions. Whether it's pursuing new opportunities, hiring additional staff, or adapting to changing patient needs, a healthy cash flow gives you the financial flexibility to act swiftly and confidently.

6.Patient Care: Ultimately, the importance of cash flow ties back to the quality of care you can provide to your patients. A stable cash flow ensures that you can invest in state-of-the-art equipment, retain skilled staff, and maintain a welcoming and well-equipped clinic environment, all of which contribute to superior patient experiences.

Let's discuss one more example based on the relationship between patient care and cash flow

Meet **Dr. X** and **Dr. Y**, both dedicated dentists running their own clinics:

Dr. X's clinic, "Healthy Smiles Dentistry," has been a fixture in the community for years. While he's known for his expertise and compassionate care, his cash flow has faced challenges. The clinic's equipment is ageing, and he has struggled to retain skilled staff due to budget constraints.

Written By **Dr. P. Mohan Raju**

One day, a patient comes in with a complex dental issue that requires advanced diagnostic imaging. However, Dr. X's outdated equipment limits his ability to provide a precise diagnosis, potentially affecting the quality of care he can offer. He realizes that without addressing his clinic's financial stability, his patients may face limitations in the care they receive.

Dr. Y operates "Dental Innovations Center." He has always been meticulous in managing his clinic's finances. Thanks to a strong cash flow, he regularly invests in advanced dental technology, ensuring his clinic is well-equipped with state-of-the-art equipment. He provides his staff with competitive compensation, and the clinic's warm and welcoming environment reflects his commitment to patient comfort. When a patient presents a challenging case, Dr. Y can confidently use cutting-edge imaging equipment to make an accurate diagnosis. He has a highly trained team that works efficiently, reducing patient wait times and ensuring a smooth and comfortable experience.

In this scenario, Dr. Y's prudent cash flow management empowers him to offer the highest quality of care to his patients. In contrast, Dr. X's clinic faces limitations in patient care due to financial constraints. This story underscores how financial stability, supported by cash flow, directly impacts a dentist's ability to provide superior patient care, and highlights the importance of financial management in the field of dentistry.

In summary, understanding the pivotal role of cash flow in your dental clinic is the foundation for effective financial management. It highlights the necessity of not just monitoring your clinic's finances but also proactively managing them to ensure consistent cash flow. By doing so, you can secure the financial stability needed to provide excellent patient care and set the stage for clinic growth and success.

Written By **Dr. P. Mohan Raju**

Chapter 2: Assess Your Current Cash Flow

Before you can effectively manage and optimize your dental clinic's cash flow, you need to begin with a comprehensive assessment of your current financial situation. This step is crucial as it provides a baseline understanding of where your clinic stands financially and helps identify potential areas for improvement. Here's a more detailed explanation of this point:

1.**Gather Financial Data**: Start by collecting and organizing all relevant financial data. This includes your clinic's income statements, balance sheets, and cash flow statements for the past year or more. This can be easily collected from your records, Electronic Medical Records (EMR), Patient Management Software (PMS) and the lab bills etc. This data will serve as the foundation for your assessment.

2. **Identify Income Sources**: Break down your clinic's sources of income. This includes income from patient services, insurance reimbursements, government grants (if applicable), corporate tie ups and any other revenue streams. Understanding where your money comes from is crucial for future planning.

3. **Analyse Expenses**: Examine your clinic's expenses in detail. Categorise them into fixed and variable expenses. Fixed expenses are consistent month-to-month, such as rent, staff salaries, electricity bills, maintenance, EMI / Loans etc. While variable expenses may fluctuate, like Dental material supplies, lab bills and staff expenses. This analysis will reveal where your money is going.

4. **Cash Flow Statement**: Create a cash flow statement or review an existing one. This document tracks the movement of cash into and out of your clinic during a specific period. It will provide insights into how cash is generated and used in your clinic. This acts as an eye opener for the way where your hard earned money goes.

5. **Assess Accounts Receivable**: Evaluate your accounts receivable, which represents the money patients owe for services rendered. Determine the average time it takes for patients to settle their bills and the percentage of uncollected payments. Timely monitor the unpaid dues and take action to collect them as soon as possible to increase your cash flow

6. **Identify Cash Flow Patterns**: Look for patterns in your cash flow. Is there a particular season or time of the month when cash flow is stronger or weaker? **Understanding these patterns can help you plan for future financial needs**.

Written By **Dr. P. Mohan Raju**

7. **Compare Projections to Reality**: Compare your past financial projections to your actual financial performance. If there are discrepancies, investigate the reasons behind them. This exercise can reveal areas where your financial planning may need adjustment.

8. **Engage with Financial Professionals**: Consider involving financial professionals, such as accountants or financial advisors, to assist in the assessment process. Their expertise can provide valuable insights into your clinic's financial health.

9. **Financial Ratios**: Calculate and review key financial ratios, such as the current ratio (current assets divided by current liabilities), to gauge your clinic's liquidity and ability to meet short-term financial obligations.

10. **Set Benchmarks and Goals**: Based on your assessment, establish benchmarks and financial goals. These can include improving cash flow, reducing accounts receivable ageing, or increasing profitability.

By conducting a thorough assessment of your current cash flow, you gain a clear understanding of your dental clinic's financial strengths and weaknesses. This knowledge empowers you to make informed decisions and take action to optimise your clinic's cash flow and overall financial health. It's the first step on your journey to financial mastery in the dental industry.

Chapter 3: Create a Cash Flow Forecast

A cash flow forecast is an invaluable financial tool that enables you to predict how money will move into and out of your dental clinic in the future. By creating and regularly updating a cash flow forecast, you can gain a forward-looking perspective on your clinic's financial health. Here's a more detailed explanation of this action point:

1. **Purpose of Cash Flow Forecasting**: Understand the primary purpose of a cash flow forecast, which is to anticipate the inflow and outflow of cash over a specified period (e.g., monthly or quarterly). This tool helps you plan for potential shortfalls and surpluses.

2. **Data Sources**: Gather historical financial data, including income, expenses, accounts receivable, and accounts payable. Use this data as a foundation for your cash flow forecast.

3. **Forecasting Period**: Decide on the time frame for your cash flow forecast. A typical forecast covers the next 12 months, but you can choose a shorter or longer period based on your clinic's needs and objectives.

4. **Revenue Projections**: Project your clinic's revenue by considering factors like the number of patient appointments, service fees, and insurance reimbursements. Account for seasonal variations, market trends, and any new revenue-generating initiatives.

5. **Expense Projections**: Estimate your clinic's expenses, both fixed and variable. Include costs related to staff salaries, rent, utilities, supplies, and any planned capital expenditures. It's essential to be as accurate as possible in your estimations.

6. **Accounts Receivable and Payable**: Incorporate predictions for accounts receivable (money expected from patients and insurance) and accounts payable (outstanding bills and liabilities). This ensures that you account for the timing of inflows and outflows.

7. **Review Cash Flow Patterns**: Analyse historical cash flow patterns to identify trends. For example, do you experience cash flow dips during certain months or seasons? Understanding these patterns helps refine your forecast.

8. **Risk Assessment**: Identify potential risks and uncertainties that could affect your cash flow. These could include economic downturns, changes in insurance policies, or unforeseen emergencies. Consider how to mitigate these risks in your forecast.

9. **Scenario Analysis**: Create multiple scenarios within your cash flow forecast. For example, develop a "worst-case" scenario where revenue is lower than expected and an "optimistic" scenario where revenue exceeds projections. This approach allows you to plan for various outcomes.

10. **Regular Updates**: Commit to regularly updating your cash flow forecast as new information becomes available. This should be a dynamic tool that adapts to changing circumstances and incorporates actual financial data.

11. **Use of Technology**: Consider using financial software or tools specifically designed for cash flow forecasting. These tools can streamline the process and provide more accurate predictions.

A well-structured cash flow forecast is an indispensable asset for proactive financial management. It not only helps you anticipate and prepare for financial challenges but also serves as a guide for making informed decisions about investments, staffing, and other financial matters within your dental clinic. By continuously refining your forecast, you can navigate the financial journey with greater confidence and foresight.

Chapter 4: Monitor Accounts Receivable

Written By **Dr. P. Mohan Raju**

Monitoring accounts receivable is a critical aspect of managing cash flow in a dental clinic. Accounts receivable represent the money that patients owe for services rendered, and effective management of these accounts ensures a consistent flow of income into your clinic. Here's a more detailed explanation of this point:

1. **Importance of Accounts Receivable**: Understand why accounts receivable management is crucial. A significant portion of your clinic's revenue may come from patient fees and insurance reimbursements. Monitoring these accounts is essential for steady cash flow.

2. **Clear Billing and Payment Policies**: Establish clear and transparent billing and payment policies for your clinic. Patients should be aware of their financial responsibilities, including copayments, deductibles, and any out-of-pocket expenses.

Let's have a detailed example in this context. Here's scenario that highlights the significance of clear billing and payment policies in a dental clinic:

The Johnson Family's Dental Visit:
The Johnson family, comprised of parents Emily and James and their two children, Lily and Max, regularly visits "Healthy Teeth Dental Care," a local dental clinic. Their experiences with the clinic's billing and payment policies illustrate the importance of transparency:

Previous Visit with Confusion:
During their previous visit, the Johnsons had experienced some confusion regarding their bill. The clinic had introduced a new service for advanced teeth cleaning, and Emily, who had opted for this service, was unsure about the associated costs.

Improved Transparency:
For their most recent visit, "Healthy Teeth Dental Care" had made significant improvements to its billing and payment policies. The Johnsons were pleasantly surprised. Here's how the scenario played out:

- Pre-Visit Information: In advance of their appointment, the Johnsons received a detailed email from the clinic, outlining their upcoming services, estimated costs, and the family's financial responsibilities. Emily and James were impressed by the clinic's proactive approach.

Written By **Dr. P. Mohan Raju**

- Itemized Bill: After their appointment, the Johnsons received an itemized bill that clearly listed the services provided, their costs, and the portions covered by their insurance. Emily could easily identify the cost of her advanced teeth cleaning, and there was no confusion.
- Copayment Explanation: The bill also explained that the Johnsons were responsible for a copayment. This copayment had been clearly discussed in their pre-visit email, so there were no unexpected surprises.
- Multiple Payment Options: The clinic offered various payment options, including online payments, and even provided a link to their secure online portal for easy payment processing. The Johnsons appreciated the flexibility.
- Insurance Verification: The clinic had verified the Johnsons' insurance coverage and accurately applied the benefits to their bill. Emily and James were relieved to see that the insurance had covered the expected portion of their dental treatments.
- Informed Decision-Making: In previous visits, Emily had opted for additional treatments without a full understanding of the costs. This time, she felt confident in her decision and had agreed to the advanced teeth cleaning after reviewing the treatment plan.
- Questions Addressed: During the visit, the Johnsons took the opportunity to ask questions about their insurance coverage and the clinic's billing process. The clinic's financial coordinator was readily available to provide answers and reassurance.

This scenario demonstrates the positive impact of clear and transparent billing and payment policies. "Healthy Teeth Dental Care" not only improved its billing communication but also empowered its patients, the Johnsons, to make informed decisions and understand their financial responsibilities. The family left the clinic feeling satisfied, informed, and confident in their choice of dental care provider.

3. **Timely Billing**: Implement a systematic process for generating and sending bills to patients and insurance providers promptly. Delays in billing can lead to delayed payments and cash flow disruptions.

4. **Insurance Verification**: Verify patients' insurance coverage before providing services. This helps ensure that the clinic will receive reimbursements for covered treatments and reduces the risk of billing disputes. This is new in India but in near future most of the insurance companies will come forward to provide insurance services for dental patients.

Written By **Dr. P. Mohan Raju**

5. **Effective Coding and Documentation**: Accurate coding and detailed documentation of patient visits are essential for insurance claims. Errors or omissions can result in claim denials, delaying reimbursements.

6. **Patient Payment Options**: Offer multiple payment options to patients, including credit card payments, online payments, and payment plans. Providing flexibility can encourage prompt payments.

7. **Ageing Reports**: Regularly review aging reports, which categorize outstanding accounts by the length of time they have been unpaid. These reports help you identify overdue accounts and take appropriate action.

8. **Follow-Up Procedures**: Establish a systematic follow-up process for unpaid accounts. Send reminders, statements, or even consider using any other modes for overdue accounts if necessary.

9. **Appeal Denied Claims**: When insurance claims are denied, ensure that your clinic has a process for appealing these denials. Insurance providers sometimes make errors that can be corrected.

10. **Regular Reconciliation**: Reconcile your accounts receivable regularly to ensure that the amount in your records matches what you expect to receive. This reconciliation process helps identify discrepancies.

11. **Patient Communication**: Maintain open communication with patients regarding their outstanding balances. Empathetic and clear communication can help resolve payment issues amicably.

Certainly, let's see an example that demonstrates the significance of clear and empathetic patient communication in a dental clinic:

The Smith Family's Outstanding Balance:

The Smith family, consisting of parents Sarah and Michael, along with their teenage daughter, Emma, have been loyal patients of "Sunshine Dental Care" for years. However, during one of their routine check-ups, they learned that they had an outstanding balance for Emma's recent orthodontic treatment. This scenario illustrates the clinic's approach to patient communication:

Initial Patient Communication:

      A. <u>Proactive Approach</u>: Sunshine Dental Care's administrative team takes a proactive approach. Instead of waiting for the Smiths to inquire about their outstanding balance, they send a friendly email to Sarah, explaining that there is an unpaid balance related to Emma's orthodontic care.

      B. <u>Empathetic Tone</u>: The email starts with a compassionate tone, acknowledging that managing healthcare expenses can sometimes be challenging. It reassures the Smiths that the clinic is here to help.

      C. <u>Clear Communication</u>: The email provides an itemized breakdown of the outstanding balance, including details of the orthodontic procedures, insurance coverage, and the patient's responsibility. The language used is plain and straightforward, avoiding any complex billing terminology.

Offering Payment Options:

<u>Payment Plan Options</u>: Sunshine Dental Care outlines several payment plan options in the email. These options accommodate different financial situations, from paying the balance in full to spreading it over several months. The terms and conditions are clearly explained.

<u>Transparency</u>: The email emphasizes that the clinic is committed to transparency. It provides a link to the clinic's billing and payment policies, so the Smiths can understand how the billing process works.

Follow-Up and Resolution:

<u>Follow-Up Reminders</u>: After a week, the clinic sends a friendly reminder email to ensure the Smiths don't forget about their outstanding balance. This reminder is not forceful but gently prompts action.

Written By **Dr. P. Mohan Raju**

Resolution Path: The email provides contact information for the clinic's financial coordinator, Lisa, and encourages the Smiths to reach out if they have any questions or concerns. The Smiths feel confident that they have a clear path to resolve any issues.

Feedback Gathering and Trust:

Feedback Gathering: In the follow-up reminder, the clinic requests feedback on the billing and communication process. The Smiths appreciate that the clinic values their input.

Privacy and Confidentiality: Sunshine Dental Care reassures the Smiths that their financial information is kept confidential and that the clinic adheres to strict privacy standards.

The Smiths, upon receiving the proactive and empathetic communication from Sunshine Dental Care, feel heard and understood. They appreciate the transparency and options offered to address their outstanding balance. This positive experience not only helps resolve the payment issue amicably but also strengthens the trust and goodwill between the Smiths and their dental care provider. Effective patient communication, as demonstrated in this scenario, is a crucial aspect of successful dental clinic management.

12. **Staff Training**: Train your staff to understand the importance of accounts receivable management and provide them with the skills to handle billing and payment-related tasks effectively.

13. **Leverage Technology**: Consider using dental practice management software that includes billing and accounts receivable management features. These tools can streamline the process and reduce errors.

14. **Financial Policies Review**: Regularly review your clinic's financial policies and make adjustments as needed to ensure they align with best practices and industry standards.

Monitoring accounts receivable is an ongoing process that requires diligence and attention to detail. By managing these accounts effectively, you can minimize the risk of cash flow disruptions, improve revenue collection, and maintain financial stability in your dental clinic.

Chapter 5: Expense Management

Effective expense management is a fundamental component of maintaining a healthy cash flow in your dental clinic. It involves systematically controlling and optimizing the costs associated with running your practice. Here's a more detailed explanation of this action point:

1. **Categorize Expenses**: Start by categorizing your clinic's expenses into fixed and variable categories. Fixed expenses, like rent and staff salaries, remain relatively constant. Variable expenses, such as supplies and utilities, fluctuate based on your clinic's activity.

2. **Expense Analysis**: Analyze your clinic's historical expenses to understand spending patterns. This can help you identify areas where cost-saving measures can be implemented without compromising patient care.

3. **Budget Development**: Create a detailed budget for your clinic that outlines the expected income and expenses for the upcoming period, typically on a monthly or annual basis. A well-structured budget provides a roadmap for financial management.

4. **Cost Reduction Strategies**: Explore opportunities for reducing costs without compromising the quality of patient care. This could involve renegotiating vendor contracts, seeking competitive quotes, or adopting more cost-effective procurement practices.

5. **Technology and Automation**: Consider adopting practice management software and technology solutions that can automate administrative tasks, streamline operations, and reduce the need for manual labour.

6. **Staffing Efficiency**: Evaluate your staffing levels and consider whether there are opportunities to optimize staff schedules or cross-train employees to perform multiple roles. This can help maximize workforce efficiency.

7. **Supplier Negotiations**: Negotiate with suppliers and vendors to secure better terms, discounts, or extended payment schedules. These negotiations can result in significant cost savings.

8. **Energy Efficiency**: Implement energy-efficient practices and technologies within your clinic to reduce utility costs. Simple measures like LED lighting and energy-efficient appliances can make a difference. Usage of low power consuming monitors/ efficient low power and high battery life laptops etc. Reduce the energy wastage and use energy efficient fridges / AC in your clinic to save utility bills.

Written By **Dr. P. Mohan Raju**

9. **Inventory Control**: Implement an inventory management system to monitor and control the levels of dental supplies and equipment. Prevent overstocking or running out of critical supplies.

10. **Regular Expense Reviews**: Continuously review your clinic's expenses to ensure that they align with your budget and financial goals. This practice can help identify cost overruns and areas for improvement.

11. **Sustainability Initiatives**: Consider sustainable practices, such as reducing paper usage, recycling, and minimizing waste. These initiatives can benefit both the environment and your clinic's bottom line. One best example from my own practice is, use autocalvable water glasses instead of regular paper/plastic glasses which will be environmental friendly and economical too.

12. **Benchmarking**: Compare your clinic's expenses with industry benchmarks to determine if your spending is in line with best practices. This benchmarking process can reveal areas for improvement.

13. **Legal and Regulatory Complianc**e: Stay informed about changes in healthcare and financial regulations that may impact your clinic's expenses. Compliance is essential for avoiding legal issues.

14. **Contingency Planning**: Develop contingency plans for unexpected expenses, such as equipment breakdowns or emergency repairs. Having financial reserves set aside for contingencies can prevent cash flow disruptions.

Effective expense management is an ongoing process that requires careful planning, monitoring, and adaptability. By proactively managing your clinic's expenses, you can ensure that your cash flow remains stable and your financial health is protected.

Chapter 6: Establish Financial Controls

Financial controls are the systematic practices and policies put in place to safeguard the financial health of your dental clinic, prevent fraud, and ensure that financial resources are used efficiently and responsibly. Here's a more detailed explanation of this action point:

1. **Control Framework**: Begin by establishing a financial control framework for your clinic. This framework should include written policies and procedures that outline how financial transactions are managed and monitored.

2. **Segregation of Duties**: Implement the segregation of duties to prevent any single individual from having too much control over financial processes. For example, the staff member responsible for approving expenses should not be the same person who processes payments.

3. **Authorization Protocols**: Develop clear authorization protocols for financial transactions. For instance, specify who can approve purchases, sign checks, or authorize budget allocations.

4. **Expense Approval Procedures**: Define the process for approving expenses, which may involve requiring staff to submit expense reports for review and approval before reimbursement.

5. **Receipt and Documentation**: Ensure that all financial transactions, including expenses and income, are properly documented. This includes retaining receipts, invoices, and supporting documents for audits and reference.

6. **Financial Reporting**: Regularly produce and review financial reports to monitor your clinic's financial performance. These reports should provide insights into income, expenses, and cash flow.

7. **Internal Audits**: Schedule periodic internal audits to review financial practices, transactions, and compliance with financial policies. Internal audits help identify any irregularities or areas for improvement.

8. **Access Controls**: Control access to financial data and systems. Limit access to authorized personnel and use technology solutions like password protection and encryption to secure financial information.

9. **Bank Reconciliations**: Reconcile your clinic's bank statements with your financial records regularly to identify any discrepancies or errors in your accounts.

10. **Budget Adherence**: Ensure adherence to the budget by tracking expenses against the budgeted amounts. Deviations from the budget should be investigated and addressed promptly.

11. **Emergency Funds**: Maintain an emergency fund or cash reserve to cover unexpected expenses, emergencies, or cash flow shortfalls. Having a financial buffer reduces the risk of financial crises.

12. **Training and Education**: Invest in the training and education of your clinic's staff regarding financial controls and best practices. Well-informed employees are better equipped to maintain financial discipline.

13. **Regulatory Compliance**: Stay informed about changes in financial regulations that may affect your clinic. Compliance with financial and healthcare regulations is crucial to avoid legal issues.

14. **Whistleblower Policies**: Establish clear whistleblower policies that allow employees to report financial irregularities or unethical behavior without fear of retaliation.

15. **External Audits**: Consider hiring external auditors or consultants to conduct periodic financial audits and reviews. External audits provide an independent assessment of your clinic's financial controls.

Establishing and maintaining strong financial controls is essential for protecting your clinic's financial assets, ensuring the integrity of financial transactions, and maintaining the trust of patients and stakeholders. It also helps mitigate the risk of fraud and legal issues, ultimately contributing to the long-term financial stability of your dental practice.

Chapter 7: Plan for Seasonal Variations

Dental clinics often experience seasonal variations in patient volume and revenue. Preparing for and managing these fluctuations is essential for maintaining consistent cash flow and financial stability. Here's a more detailed explanation of this context

Written By **Dr. P. Mohan Raju**

1. **Understanding Seasonal Variations**: Recognize that dental clinics may have busier and slower seasons. For example, many clinics see increased patient traffic during the back-to-school season or after the holiday period, these trends vary from clinic to clinic and location to location. Identify the seasonal trends / variations in cash flow. The only person who can judge the seasonal variation of your clinic is YOU!

Seasonal variation trends are not so easily identified, it requires atleast two years of back data of your income, expenses, patient flow to clearly analyse and predict them.

2. **Historical Data Analysis**: Analyze historical data to identify patterns in patient volume and revenue associated with different times of the year. This analysis helps you anticipate upcoming seasonal variations.

3. **Budget Adjustments**: Develop a budget that takes into account the expected fluctuations in patient volume. Allocate resources, such as staff hours and marketing efforts, to align with anticipated demand.

4. **Marketing Strategies**: Implement marketing strategies that capitalize on seasonal trends. For example, you might run special promotions or campaigns during periods of increased patient activity. Better patient engagement is the key for increased patient flow and increased cash flow.

5. **Staff Scheduling**: Create flexible staff schedules that can be adjusted to accommodate changing patient volume. Cross-training employees allows for more agile workforce management.

6. **Cash Flow Projections**: Develop cash flow projections that account for both peak and off-peak seasons. This can help you anticipate cash flow surpluses and shortfalls.

7. **Patient Retention**: Focus on patient retention strategies to maintain a consistent patient base. Encourage regular check-ups and build relationships with patients to ensure their loyalty year-round.

8. **Financial Reserves**: Consider setting aside financial reserves during peak seasons to help cover expenses during slower periods. These reserves act as a financial buffer against cash flow disruptions.

Written By **Dr. P. Mohan Raju**

9. **Expense Control**: During peak seasons, when revenue is higher, be cautious not to increase expenses excessively. Maintain disciplined cost control practices to preserve profitability.

10. **Community Engagement**: Engage with your local community during slow seasons. Participate in community events, offer free educational seminars, or engage in outreach to attract new patients. Organise Dental camps and promotional events to attract more patients

11. **Emergency Planning**: Develop contingency plans for unforeseen circumstances that may disrupt seasonal patterns, such as a sudden decrease in patient volume due to a public health crisis.

12. **Data-Driven Decision-Making**: Use data and analytics to make informed decisions. Track the effectiveness of your strategies and adjust your approach based on the results.

13. **Cash Flow Optimization**: When experiencing high revenue during peak seasons, aim to optimize cash flow by promptly processing insurance claims and ensuring timely collections.

Planning for seasonal variations is crucial for maintaining steady cash flow and avoiding financial stress during slow periods. By analyzing historical data, adjusting budgets, and implementing proactive strategies, your dental clinic can manage these fluctuations effectively, ensuring long-term financial stability.

Chapter 8: Explore Revenue Diversification

Revenue diversification is the practice of expanding your clinic's income sources beyond the traditional patient fees. It involves exploring additional revenue streams and strategies to enhance financial stability and resilience. Here's a more detailed explanation of this action point:

Written By **Dr. P. Mohan Raju**

1. **Rationale for Diversification**: Understand the need for revenue diversification in dental clinic management. Relying solely on patient fees can make your clinic vulnerable to fluctuations in patient volume and changes in insurance policies.

2. **New Services and Specializations**: Consider offering additional dental services or specializations that align with your clinic's expertise and patient demand. For instance, you might introduce orthodontics, cosmetic dentistry, or oral surgery.

3. **Partnerships and Collaborations**: Explore partnerships with other healthcare providers, such as general practitioners, oral surgeons, or specialists. Collaborative care can attract new patients and create cross-referral opportunities.

4. **Telehealth and Remote Consultations**: Embrace telehealth and virtual consultations, particularly for non-emergency services. Offering remote consultations can expand your reach and revenue potential.

5. **Dental Technology Investments**: Invest in advanced dental technologies and equipment that can enable new services, improve patient care, and attract a broader patient base.

6. **Membership Plans**: Create membership or subscription plans that provide patients with ongoing dental care for a fixed fee. These plans can enhance patient loyalty and provide a steady source of income.

7. **Insurance Network Expansion**: Consider expanding your participation in insurance networks or collaborating with multiple providers. This can increase the number of patients who can access your clinic's services.

8. **Patient Education and Preventive Care**: Emphasize patient education and preventive care programs to reduce the need for complex and costly treatments. This can lead to more predictable revenue from regular check-ups and cleanings.

9. **Community Engagement**: Engage with your local community through educational programs, outreach events, and partnerships with schools and organizations. These efforts can introduce your clinic to potential patients.

10. **International Patients**: Explore the potential to attract international patients for specialized treatments or dental tourism. Provide information in multiple languages and facilitate patient travel and accommodation arrangements.

11. **Private Pay and Financing Options**: Offer flexible private pay options and financing plans to accommodate patients who may not have insurance or prefer alternative payment methods.

12. **Marketing and Branding**: Develop a marketing and branding strategy that highlights your clinic's unique services and strengths. Effective branding can differentiate your clinic in a competitive market.

13. **Data-Driven Decision-Making**: Use data analytics to assess the effectiveness of your diversification strategies. Track the performance of new services and revenue streams to make informed decisions.

14. **Risk Assessment**: Assess the risks and potential challenges associated with revenue diversification, and have contingency plans in place to mitigate these risks.

Diversifying your clinic's revenue sources can make it more resilient to market fluctuations, enhance financial stability, and provide opportunities for growth. By strategically expanding the services you offer and exploring new revenue streams, you can position your clinic for long-term success in a dynamic healthcare environment.

Chapter 9: Build a Financial Buffer

Building a financial buffer involves setting aside funds specifically designed to cover unexpected expenses, emergencies, and cash flow shortfalls. This reserve acts as a financial safety net and is a critical element of prudent financial management for your dental clinic. Here's a more detailed explanation of this action point:

1. **Purpose of a Financial Buffer**: Understand the primary purpose of a financial buffer, which is to provide your dental clinic with financial stability and resilience. It serves as a safety net that can be accessed in times of need.

2. **Emergency Fund Basics**: An emergency fund is a designated savings account that holds a sum of money to cover unexpected expenses or emergencies. It should be easily accessible but separate from your regular operational accounts.

3. **Determining the Fund Size**: Assess your clinic's specific financial situation to determine the appropriate size of your financial buffer. Many financial experts recommend saving three to six months' worth of expenses.

4. **Regular Contributions**: Set a budget to make regular contributions to your financial buffer. These contributions can be made on a monthly or quarterly basis, depending on your clinic's financial performance.

5. **Types of Expenses Covered**: Your financial buffer can be used to cover a wide range of unexpected expenses, including equipment repairs, urgent maintenance, unexpected staff leave, or cash flow shortfalls during slow periods.

6. **Strategic Planning**: Strategically allocate funds to your financial buffer based on the clinic's needs. For instance, you might allocate a larger portion during a profitable period to prepare for upcoming lean months.

7. **Separate Account**: Create a separate savings or investment account for your financial buffer. It should be distinct from your regular operating accounts to prevent unintentional spending.

8. **Risk Management**: Identify and assess potential risks that could lead to unexpected financial challenges. Common risks include equipment breakdowns, economic downturns, or extended staff absences.

9. **Asset Liquidity**: Ensure that your financial buffer consists of liquid assets that can be accessed quickly when needed. Avoid tying up these funds in long-term investments or assets.

Written By **Dr. P. Mohan Raju**

10. **Regular Review**: Periodically review the size and status of your financial buffer to ensure that it aligns with your clinic's financial objectives and the changing economic landscape.

11. **Tax Considerations**: Be aware of any tax implications associated with your financial buffer, such as potential tax benefits or consequences of using these funds.

12. **Financial Advisor Guidance**: Consult with a financial advisor or professional to determine the optimal strategies for building and managing your financial buffer.

13. **Contingency Planning**: Develop contingency plans that outline how your financial buffer will be utilized in specific emergency scenarios. Having a clear plan in place helps you respond swiftly to financial challenges.

Let me explain with an example. In this scenario at "Bright Smiles Dental Clinic," Dr. Sarah Anderson, an experienced dentist and clinic owner, takes deliberate steps to ensure financial resilience for her practice. She comprehends that unforeseen challenges, such as equipment breakdowns or unexpected staff absences, can disrupt clinic operations and patient care. With a clear understanding of the primary purpose of a financial buffer, she establishes an emergency fund, distinct from the regular operational accounts, and commits to building a buffer that covers six months' worth of clinic expenses.

Monthly contributions and strategic planning further fortify this fund, which can be utilized to address various unforeseen expenses, including equipment repairs. Dr. Anderson's commitment to maintaining a separate account, identifying potential risks, and regularly reviewing the fund's status underscores her dedication to financial stability. Her collaboration with a financial advisor and the development of contingency plans highlight her meticulous approach to financial management, ensuring that "Bright Smiles Dental Clinic" can confidently face unexpected challenges while upholding its commitment to providing exceptional patient care.

Building a financial buffer is an essential part of responsible financial management for your dental clinic. It ensures that you have the resources necessary to navigate unexpected financial hurdles without jeopardizing your clinic's stability or the quality of patient care. It provides peace of mind and flexibility to focus on long-term growth and success.

Written By **Dr. P. Mohan Raju**

Chapter 10: Continuously Improve Financial Literacy

Financial literacy is the foundation of effective financial management for a dental clinic. Continuously improving your financial literacy, as well as that of your staff, is essential for making informed decisions, optimizing cash flow, and ensuring the long-term financial health of your clinic. Here's a more detailed explanation of this action point:

1. **The Value of Financial Literacy**: Understand why financial literacy is vital for your clinic's success. It enables you to make informed financial decisions, navigate complex financial landscapes, and identify opportunities for improvement.

2. **Continuous Learning Culture**: Cultivate a culture of continuous learning within your clinic. Encourage staff members to seek ongoing education and training related to financial management.

3. **Educational Resources**: Access a wide range of educational resources, such as books, articles, webinars, courses, and workshops, to improve your financial literacy. Many resources are specifically tailored to healthcare professionals.

4. **Staff Training and Development**: Invest in the financial literacy of your staff, particularly those involved in financial processes. Providing training on financial topics ensures that they understand their roles in managing the clinic's finances.

5. **Professional Associations**: Join and participate in dental and healthcare professional associations and networks that offer financial education, resources, and peer support.

6. **Financial Advisors**: Establish relationships with financial advisors, accountants, or financial consultants who can provide expert guidance and insights into financial best practices.

7. **Accounting and Financial Software**: Utilize accounting and financial management software to streamline financial processes, track financial data, and generate reports. Familiarize yourself and your staff with these tools.

8. **Benchmarking and Industry Standards**: Stay informed about industry standards and benchmarks for financial performance in the dental field. This knowledge helps you assess how your clinic compares to peers.

9. **Case Studies and Best Practices**: Study case studies and best practices from successful dental clinics that excel in financial management. Learn from their experiences and apply relevant strategies to your clinic.

Written By **Dr. P. Mohan Raju**

10. **Financial Metrics**: Gain proficiency in key financial metrics that are relevant to your clinic, such as profitability ratios, liquidity ratios, and efficiency ratios. These metrics provide insights into your clinic's financial health.

11. **Budgeting and Forecasting**: Develop expertise in budgeting and cash flow forecasting. These tools are essential for setting financial goals and making informed decisions about resource allocation.

12. **Risk Management and Compliance**: Enhance your knowledge of risk management strategies and compliance with financial regulations. Ensure that your clinic's financial practices align with legal requirements.

13. **Professional Development Plans**: Create individualized professional development plans for yourself and your staff. These plans should outline the specific areas of financial literacy that need improvement and the steps to achieve that improvement.

14. **Regular Assessment**: Continuously assess your financial literacy and that of your staff. Regular self-assessment and performance evaluations help identify areas that require further attention.

15. **Mentorship and Coaching**: Seek mentorship or coaching from experienced financial professionals or mentors within the healthcare industry. Learning from their experiences can accelerate your financial knowledge.

Improving financial literacy is an ongoing journey that should be a priority in your dental clinic's operations. With a commitment to learning, staying up-to-date with industry changes, and proactively seeking education and guidance, you can navigate the complexities of dental finance with confidence and precision. Financial literacy is not just a skill; it's a cornerstone of long-term financial success in your clinic.

Conclusion

In conclusion, "Mastering Dental Clinic Cash Flow," has provided a comprehensive foundation for effective financial management in the field of dentistry. We have explored ten key action points that collectively form the blueprint for optimizing cash flow and ensuring the long-term financial health of your dental clinic.

Written By **Dr. P. Mohan Raju**

From understanding the critical importance of cash flow to creating a cash flow forecast, monitoring accounts receivable, managing expenses, and diversifying revenue streams, we've covered essential strategies for success. We've also emphasized the significance of financial controls, planning for seasonal variations, building a financial buffer, and continuously improving financial literacy as integral components of your financial management toolkit.

As you move forward, it's essential to remember that financial management in the dental industry is not a one-time task but an ongoing commitment. By applying the principles and action points outlined in this chapter, you are setting a strong foundation for the chapters to come.

In the subsequent chapters, we will delve deeper into specific financial management strategies, explore advanced techniques for revenue optimization, and address challenges unique to the dental industry. Our goal is to empower you with the knowledge and tools you need to navigate the financial landscape confidently, ultimately enabling you to provide exceptional patient care while ensuring the financial success of your dental clinic.

We invite you to embrace these financial management principles, apply them diligently, and continue your journey toward mastering dental clinic cash flow. With dedication, continuous learning, and a commitment to financial excellence, you will not only secure the financial well-being of your clinic but also enhance your ability to provide top-quality dental care to your patients. Together, we look forward to the financial success and prosperity that lies ahead in the chapters that follow.

Written By **Dr. P. Mohan Raju**